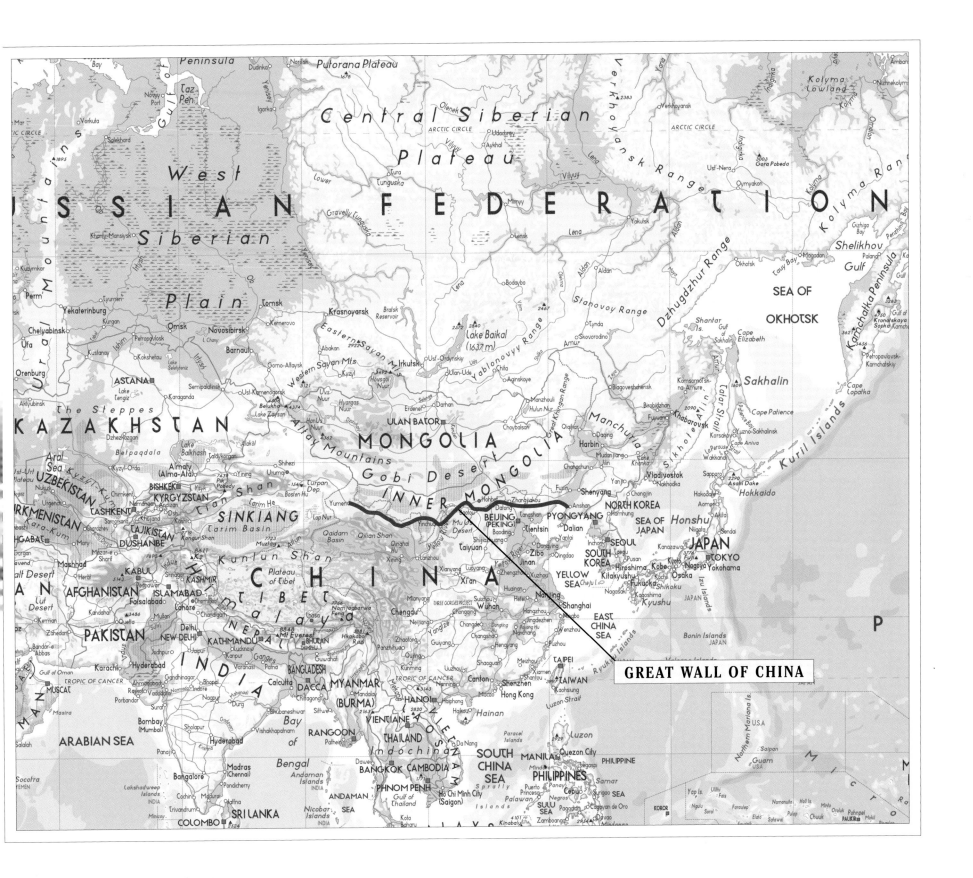

GREAT WALL OF CHINA

Published by Creative Education
123 South Broad Street
Mankato, Minnesota 56001

Creative Education is an imprint of The Creative Company.

Designed by Stephanie Blumenthal
Production design by The Design Lab
Art direction by Rita Marshall

Photographs by Corbis (Asian Art & Archaeology, Inc., John F. Albert, Morton Beebe,
Bettmann, Christie's Images, Dean Conger, Ric Ergenbright, Owen Franken, Free Agents Limited,
Freelance Consulting Services Pty Ltd, Todd A. Gipstein, Historical Picture Archive,
Wolfgang Kaehler, Jutta Klee, Bryan Knox; Papilio, George D. Lepp, Liu Liqun, Joe McDonald,
Reuters, Royalty-Free, Setboun, John Slater, Joseph Sohm; ChromoSohm Inc., Paul A. Souders,
Spaceborne Imaging Radar-C/X-Band Synthetic Aperture Radar, James Sparshatt,
Stapleton Collection, Keren Su, Nik Wheeler, Nevada Wier, Michael S. Yamashita)

Printed in the United States of America

Library of Congress Cataloging-in-Publication Data

Richardson, Adele, 1966–
Great Wall of China / by Adele Richardson.
p. cm. — (Ancient wonders of the world)
Includes index.
ISBN 1-58341-356-1
1. Great Wall of China (China)—Juvenile literature. I. Title. II. Series.

DS793.G67R53 2004   355'.7'09514—dc22   2004055265

First edition

2 4 6 8 9 7 5 3 1

Great Wall of China

A D E L E   R I C H A R D S O N

C R E A T I V E E D U C A T I O N

124510

The Great Wall is one of the largest construction projects ever completed. It rises from the country-side as a silent testament to the power of the ancient Chinese people.

On the east coast of China, the Yellow Sea laps against 75 feet (23 m) of aged stone that reaches out onto shore. Stone soon turns to brick and zigzags into the western landscape for hundreds of miles, resembling a long, thin dragon slithering across northern China with its head rest-ing in the sea. In fact, the Great Wall of China, built thousands of years ago for both defense and beauty, is often called the Sleeping Dragon. The name is appropriate, for the mythical dragon is not only a sym-bol of good luck in China, but a creature of great strength as well.

THE LAND OF WALLS

During the Warring States period, the state of Yan built one of the longest known walls. It stretched along the state's northern border for about 800 miles (1,290 km). Yan's ancient wall is thought to be one of the last built before the start of the Qin **dynasty**.

Originally built to protect crops such as rice and beans, the wall is today a landmark recognized around the world.

China has been building walls for thousands of years. About 6,000 years ago, its people were divided into many tribes. Some constantly roamed across the **arid** northern portion of the land, hunting and gathering food. Others settled in the south and began raising crops, such as rice or tea, in fertile soil. Once the tribes in the north discovered that their southern neighbors could stay in one place and still have plenty of food, some of them began raiding southern farming villages.

China's earliest walls were built around these **agricultural** villages in the south.

Historians believe that many early villages built walls for two purposes: to slow down invaders, giving villagers a chance to arm themselves or flee, and to isolate the people inside from the outside world. Without foreign influence, leaders inside the walls could have absolute authority. As village and tribal leaders grew in power, so grew the size of the lands they controlled—and the walls around them. Over the next 1,500 years, villages grew into powerful states, and the numbers of **nomadic** tribes decreased.

6

Because of their farming expertise, the ancient Chinese obtained about 90 percent of their food energy from grains and vegetables. They carved the hills of southern China into terraced rice paddies and worked the picturesque land by hand.

Building the Qin Wall was grueling work. All types of people, including slaves, criminals, soldiers, teachers, and farmers, were ordered to build it. Most workers slept on the cold ground and had no access to toilets or baths. Food became scarce because so many farmers were working on the project.

The years between 481 and 221 B.C. are known as China's Warring States Period. During this time, the land was divided into 10 or more states, each ruled by a king. The states fought violently against each other to gain access to more land and resources such as rivers, farmland, and iron deposits. Many rulers ordered increasingly long walls built along their borders to pro-tect their kingdoms from invaders. Some walls were only a few hundred feet long, while others stretched for hundreds of miles. China was quickly becom-ing a land of walls.

As each state's strength grew, the barriers along its borders increased as well. **Archaeologists** believe that at least six states—Chu, Qi, Qin, Wei, Yan, and Zhao—built giant walls that defended their kingdoms for hundreds of miles. During the fourth century B.C., Qin and Chu were the largest and strongest of all the states and waged long, bloody bat-tles against each other. Tens of thousands of soldiers died as the two states fought to gain control of all of China. By 221 B.C., Qin had emerged victorious, and King Zheng, its ruler, named himself China's first

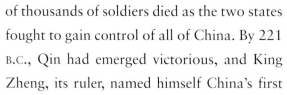

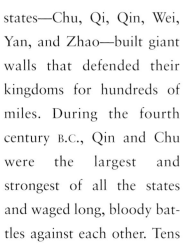

Bricks were transported to the top of the Wall by men, donkeys, and mules. Despite the lack of modern machinery, the builders of the Wall were masterful architects, as is evident in the intricate designs on the Wall's watchtowers (opposite far left). Expert craftsmanship can also be seen in the 8,000 statues (left) found in Qin Shi Huangdi's tomb.

The name Qin Shi Huangdi is pronounced *chin shee hwong-dee.* *Shi* means "first," while *Huangdi* translates as "august lord" or "emperor." Put together, the name means "first emperor of Qin," the state in which he was born. The western name "China" evolved from "chin," the pronunciation of Qin.

emperor. The Warring States Period was finally over.

Zheng, who renamed himself Qin Shi Huangdi, was a merciless ruler who maintained absolute control over his subjects and land. The emperor ordered roads built so that he could easily travel to all parts of China and keep an eye on his people. There was a key problem in his road-building plans, however: many walls built during the Warring States Period now stood as obstacles to such construction.

Qin Shi Huangdi had another problem as well. Tribes from the nation of Mongolia

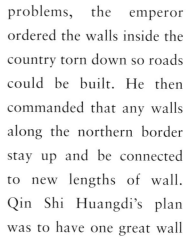

to the north were still trying to invade his country, and soldiers had to constantly guard against attacks. To solve both of his problems, the emperor ordered the walls inside the country torn down so roads could be built. He then commanded that any walls along the northern border stay up and be connected to new lengths of wall. Qin Shi Huangdi's plan was to have one great wall separate his country from the north. The giant wall would not only serve as protection against invading nomads, but also stand as a symbol of the Chinese emperor's great power.

Soldiers stationed along the Wall (opposite) served as the country's first line of defense against invaders. In order to ease travel through the treacherous terrain inside the walled territory, miles of snaking roads were cut through China's mountains.

YEARS IN THE MAKING

Sun-baked bricks were made by combining water and dirt, then pouring the mixture into wooden molds. After the bricks hardened, the molds were emptied and used to make more bricks. During the Ming dynasty, bricks were baked in kilns or ovens instead of drying in the sun.

The Great Wall of China stretches about 1,850 miles (2,980 km), from just south of the city of Shanhaiguan in the east to slightly past the city of Jiayuguan in the west. In some areas, the Wall runs along China's northern border; in other sections, it runs several hundred miles south of the border. Because the Wall includes many smaller walls that wind off from the main structure, each of which runs for 100 miles (161 km) or less, the Wall actually measures about 4,000 miles (6,440 km) in all.

China's Great Wall is not one continuous structure, but a series of walls connected to towers. When the Wall was built, archers used two bowshots to determine the spacing of towers, which meant that towers were built anywhere from 100 to 200 yards (91 to 183 m) apart. For building materials, workers used sun-baked bricks and wood from any trees that grew nearby. Evergreen trees were most commonly used, since such tree species were abundant throughout the central portion of the country. If wood was not available in an area, it was brought from miles away by horse-drawn carts. Each side of the Great Wall's towers is about 20 feet (6.1 m) wide, and the towers

Mud bricks (opposite) that were made by hand formed a solid foundation for the Wall and its many watchtowers. Soldiers that looked much like the figures (below) found in Qin Shi Huangdi's tomb took up posts in the lonely towers.

The wall Qin Shi Huangdi ordered built in 221 B.C. was a *wanli changchen*, a 10,000-li wall. A li is a Chinese measurement for distance. It is approximately 1,640 feet (500 m), or just under one-third of a mile. A 10,000-li wall measures just over 3,100 miles (4,990 km) long.

Portions of the Wall that have fallen into disrepair are restored (opposite) using the original building materials and methods.

stand about 40 feet (12.2 m) high. Once the towers were erected, the walls were built to link them together.

All parts of the Great Wall were built entirely by hand using the *hang-tu* method. The Chinese word *hang* translates as "beaten," and *tu* roughly means "earth." To build a *hang-tu* wall, workers literally beat down layers of dirt. First, a wooden form was built. Then several inches of dirt, rocks, and twigs were dumped inside of it. To **compact** the dirt and remove any air pockets, workers **tamped** it down with tools. When the wall was the desired height, the forms were removed

to reveal a strong, solid wall. The entire Great Wall was built in such a manner, although building materials varied from location to location and from dynasty to dynasty.

Historians believe that three dynasties—Qin, Han, and Ming—were involved in the Wall's creation over a period of more than 1,800 years. Although Qin Shi Huangdi ordered the original Great Wall built, he did not design it. No one knows who the original **architect** was. The Qin dynasty lasted from 221 to 206 B.C. and is credited with constructing approximately 3,000 miles (4,830 km) of the Wall. Between 206 B.C. and A.D. 220, the

The Great Wall bears inscriptions (right) dating back to when soldiers stood guard along it. While most of the Wall towers over the land, portions have been submerged in the Luan River (opposite bottom).

Han dynasty ruled China. During this time, Emperor Wu Di added another 300 miles (483 km) of western Wall that ran into the Gobi desert. Wu Di also ordered built nearly 70 miles (113 km) of unconnected **watchtowers** that extended beyond the western end. After that, no substantial work was done on the Wall for about 1,100 years.

Most of the Great Wall that remains today was built during the Ming dynasty, which lasted from A.D. 1368 to 1644. By the time Zhu Yuanzhang, the first Ming emperor, came to

power, the Wall was crumbling from neglect and **erosion**. The Ming built a new and stronger Wall and added to its overall length. The Ming Wall is actually built a slight distance south of the Qin and Han Walls' location. The Ming also used the *hang-tu* method, but with sturdier building materials. Instead of removable wooden forms, permanent stone and kiln-baked bricks were used and became part of the structure. Watchtowers were often constructed from brick, stone, and slabs of granite. The top of the Wall was paved with brick and served as a roadway for horses and Chinese soldiers.

One reason the Ming Great Wall still stands today is because rainwater drains were built into its original design. Rain seeped into the Qin and Han Walls, then froze in the winter. The expansion of the ice and subsequent melting in warm weather caused the Walls to crack and crumble.

CHINA'S SLEEPING DRAGON

The ancient Chinese were the first to discover how to manufacture silk from the cocoons of silkworms (right) and guarded their secret for nearly 2,000 years. Still considered a luxury item, silk was an important source of income for early Chinese traders.

During the Han dynasty, goods trading became very profitable for China. Other nations wanted items such as tea, spices, paper, and especially silk. Eventually, several trade routes formed in the west that merged and ran east to the Chinese city of Xi'an. The routes collectively became known as the Silk Road. A section of the Silk Road ran along the Great Wall, which enabled soldiers to protect merchants from attacks.

The Han dynasty's openness to foreigners did not last. In fact, for most of China's history, the country has been closed off to other nations. After the Ming dynasty ended in 1644, the Qing dynasty came to power and ruled until 1911. The Qing used their political power to keep China's borders closed as much as possible. For hundreds of years, most of the information gathered about the Great Wall came in the form of second-hand stories.

One particular story caused riots throughout China. In 1899, four newspaper reporters in Denver, Colorado, needed to come up with a story and didn't have one. So they made up an article that said China wanted to demolish its Great Wall. The story claimed it

20

Rising from the Gobi desert, where the temperature can change by 58 °F (32 °C) within 24 hours, the mighty Ming fortress of Jiayuguan was built at the westernmost edge of the Great Wall to guard entrance into the country.

During the 1960s, China's government decreed Chinese traditions to be old-fashioned and hateful, and it ordered that items from the country's past be destroyed. The next 20 years became known as China's Cultural Revolution. Many ancient relics were destroyed, including books, statues, and hundreds of miles of the Great Wall.

was going to be China's way of showing the world that it was opening up its borders. A newspaper in China heard the story and wrote that soldiers from America and Europe were coming to destroy the Wall. The rumor infuriated the Chinese people, who began attacking foreign **embassies** in their country. The rioting lasted for about a year and resulted in thousands of deaths.

It was not until 1972 that China once more allowed visitors. That year, Richard Nixon became the first United States President ever to visit the Great Wall. Since that historic trip, countless tourists—both dignitaries and common people—from all over the world have spent millions of dollars each year to see the Wall.

The Great Wall has long been surrounded by myths. For example, people once said that it could be seen from the moon. In fact, the Wall is not visible from the moon, but it is visible from Earth's orbit. Astronauts have to know exactly where to look, however, because despite the Wall's vast length, its thin design makes it difficult to spot.

Another subject that has been debated for years is whether bodies are buried in the Great Wall. It is unlikely that any dead are buried in the existing Ming Wall, because **decomposing**

22

Intricate carvings, such as those on temples (opposite), were among the casualties of the Cultural Revolution. Fortunately, while portions of the Great Wall also were destroyed, much of it remains intact and can be seen as an orange line in radar photographs taken in 1994 from the space shuttle Endeavour.

People of all ages enjoy visiting the Great Wall, several hundred miles of which have been carefully restored (below) using the hang-tu *method employed by the Ming more than 400 years ago. Every year, more lengths of the Wall are restored to further preserve the wonder for future generations.*

bodies would cause air pockets to form, which would have weakened the structure. Bodies may have been entombed in the long-lost Qin Wall, however. The ruthless Qin Shi Huangdi forced a large portion of the population to work on the project, and conditions were so bad that hundreds of thousands of people died. Long trenches were dug alongside the Wall and filled with the dead, which earned the Wall the nickname, "The Longest Cemetery on Earth."

By the mid-1980s, the Great Wall was China's most popular tourist attraction. In 1987, the United Nations Educational, Scientific, and Cultural Organization (UNESCO) named it a World Heritage Site, which means the site is considered culturally valuable to the world. The organization works with governments to help protect all such historic sites. That same decade, the Chinese government began restoring the Wall to strengthen it for the benefit of visitors today and in future generations.

More than 2,200 years have passed since the first Chinese emperor ordered the construction of a Great Wall. Today, China's Sleeping Dragon still slithers across the land-scape. Each brick of its body tells the story of a worker, a ruler, a dynasty, and a people. This incredible ancient structure, built to keep invaders out and secrets in, is today one of the most marvelous wonders of the world.

SEEING THE WONDER

Millions of people visit the Great Wall every year. One of the most popular tourist destinations is the Badaling section of the Wall, which is less than 45 miles (73 km) from Beijing, China's capital city. Badaling is one of the best-preserved Wall sites and can be very crowded during holidays and the peak of the tourist season. Returning visitors often recommend visiting this section early in the day to avoid the crowds. Visitors need to be aware of their own fitness and health, as the stairs leading up to the site are very steep.

Most people visiting the Great Wall do so in group tours. Travel packages usually include airfare to and from China, hotels, transportation, meals, **visa** arrangements, and experienced, English-speaking guides. The most popular tourist sites in Beijing and at the Wall announce the time and bus schedules in English for those who decide to explore away from a group. Travelers can choose from many different tour packages, which range from several days to several weeks.

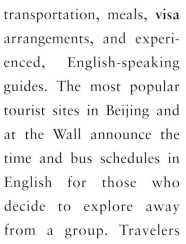

While some portions of the Wall have been turned into tourist attractions or defaced by graffiti (opposite), other areas remain relatively untouched by the modern world. Today, China is working to find a balance between development and protection.

Cool mountain winds provide natural air-conditioning inside the watchtowers, some of which can also serve as overnight camping spots for the adventurous tourist. From these high perches, one can almost see history unfolding along the Wall's vast length.

The best times of year to visit the Wall are spring and early fall, when daytime highs reach 68 to 86 °F (20–30 °C). July and August make up China's rainy season. Nights can be cold, so visitors are encouraged to bring some warm clothing. Researching the climate at the portion of the Wall you will be visiting is a must, because the structure stretches through three distinct geographic regions. The eastern section of the Wall extends across steep mountains that can become very windy. The central part runs through arid **steppes** of sandy soil, and the westernmost portion lies in ruins in the hot Gobi desert.

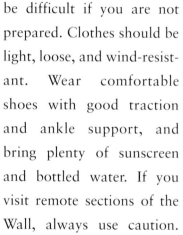

Walking and hiking the Great Wall can be difficult if you are not prepared. Clothes should be light, loose, and wind-resistant. Wear comfortable shoes with good traction and ankle support, and bring plenty of sunscreen and bottled water. If you visit remote sections of the Wall, always use caution. Never climb on any parts that look unstable; doing so could injure you or damage the Wall. Lastly, before traveling to the Great Wall or any foreign destination, check travel safety warnings for severe weather, health, or political issues that may affect your trip.

Although many of the Great Wall's steps are steep, a climb to the highest watchtowers, which in places sit at an elevation of 3,300 feet (1,000 m), provides an unequaled view of the land that is home to this 2,000-year-old piece of Chinese history.

GREAT WALL  OF CHINA

QUICK FACTS

Location: Northern China

Age: Ming Wall is more than 400 years old; some existing relics of Qin and Han Walls date back more than 2,000 years

Length: ~ 4,000 miles (6,440 km), including sections branching off from the main structure

Average width: 21 feet (6.4 m) at base, 19 feet (5.8 m) at top

Average height: 26 feet (7.9 m)

Average watchtower dimensions: 20 feet (6.1 m) long and 40 feet (12.2 m) high

Composition: Mostly dirt, stone, granite, and brick

Builders: People of China during the Qin, Han, and Ming dynasties

Number of workers who died during construction: Estimates range from 400,000 to more than 1 million

Geographic setting: Extends through deserts, steppes, and mountains, and ends at the Yellow Sea

Native plant life: Includes desert grasslands and shrubs, and various species of evergreen trees

Native animal life: Includes wild horses, foxes, wolves, leopards, gazelles, lizards, and pheasants

Other Names: *Wanli Changchen* (the 10,000-li Wall), The Sleeping Dragon, The Longest Cemetery on Earth

agricultural—related to the practice of growing crops

archaeologists—scientists who learn about the past by digging up and studying old structures or objects

architect—a person who designs buildings and other structures and oversees their construction

arid—extremely dry; a term that describes land that receives little rainfall

compact—to press together to make something more dense; workers pressed dirt and stone together to give the Great Wall a dense center

decomposing—rotting or decaying; all living things decompose after they die

dynasty—a series of powerful rulers who all belong to the same family

embassies—places in a country where representatives from other countries live and work

erosion—the gradual wearing away of something by wind and water

historians—people who learn about, study, and write about the past

nomadic—a term that describes people who roam from place to place, often to find food

steppes—large areas of dry, flat land that have few or no trees

tamped—driven down firmly; workers building the Great Wall tamped layers of dirt with tools to remove air pockets

visa—an official document that gives a person permission to enter a foreign country

watchtowers—tall buildings used by soldiers to watch over people or spot enemies